Through the Eye of a Crow

Julie Boden

Pontefract Press

2003

Publisher: Pontefract Press
                        17 Linden Terrace
                        Pontefract
                        WF8 4AE
                        Telephone: 01977 793121

©Text: Julie Boden

Cover design: Jake Schühle-Lewis, *Clockwork Sheep*

Book design: Reini Schühle and Brian Lewis, Pontefract Press

Publication date: Summer 2003

ISBN: 1 900325 34 9

For my Mother and my Father
always with Love

CONTENTS

Creation songs

Songs of Man

Prolegomenon

Do we weave our dreams
or dreams weave us?

CROW DANCE

Waddling the apple of the
earth

he pecks
and steps
and pecks
and cocks his head.

A small black radar
set to hear faint echoes
of the primal bang,
the bubbling of
quantum foam
the rising of a movement in
the worm.

He blocks his own thoughts first
then blocks the thoughts
of men
and animals
and birds
all living things
and then the high-low whistle
of the train,
revving cars,
distant thoughts,
small stone memories.

His yellow eye
is falling in a trance.

His breath
a frozen snowflake in the air
waits and hangs
in
space.

And then he hears the
movement of the worm.
He steps
and pecks
and stops
and pecks
again.

He beats
a crow beak-crow feet
strange rain dance
to call the worm
and when it comes
remembers his mistake.

This time he does not peck
the worm in two:
the woman
and
the man

This time he seeks no
knowledge from the worm.
Nothing is created
from this call
except a hole
that crow
can look
into

except a large worm hole
a hole that fits his eye
his yellow eye
that stares through
space and time

that rides the surfboard
of an ancient foam

a yellow staring eye
that learns the secrets of
some far off place
and brings them back.

He holds the watcher
with his staring eye
his pupil opens up a large
black hole
that sucks my senses in to see
those far off things
to share the numbing sorrow
of his watch.

He pecks the frozen field of
feathered ground
a car park covered in an
Angel's frost and iron stone.

We wonder why the
wormhole starts to eat
as knowledge of the crow
eats us alive
we wonder why
the wormhole starts to eat.

Worm Song

A vortex
a vortex sucking darkness
a vortex sucking darkness
spewing light

eating
eating, churning,
eating, churning matter,
turning, churning matter,
churning, turning matter
like a worm.

Gobbling
Gobbling nothingness
Gobbling a nothingness
Gobbling all nothingness
Gobbinguniversalnothingness
Gobbing out the stars that fill
the night. The gobbing of
globular constellations.

The worm moves on
the worm moves on into a
blackened soil

The worm moves on
in ever blackened soil.

Her holes leave constellations
in their wake.

Constellations spinning
in her wake

Aeons long in labour
she moves on

Aeons long in labour
she moves on and
pushes

Pushes out the pain of it.

Through each strong contraction

she moves on

pushes on

and pushes.

Pushes out

the pain of it.

Through each strong contraction
she moves on
and pushes
pushes,
pushes,
pushes,
pushes
on.

Once upon a time
there was a worm.

Once upon a time
there was a worm
crow split   in two.

Once upon a time
there was a worm.
A mighty worm that spewed
creation up.

Once upon a time
there was a worm
that spewed
the whole creation up
and tired from all her labour
now she sleeps.

Trapped between the
tea and toast of sleep.

Trapped inside the veils
of pethidine.

Dreamily
she digs a place to rest
half sleeping and half dreaming
turning in her, churning in her sleep.
She eats the stars
turns blackness
into light,
sleeps inside the labours
of her love,
half aware the stars
are moving out,
half aware that there has been
a birth,
half awake to hear
creation call -
the screaming of her baby
in the night.
Knowing only something
of herself
she hears that separate
sound
that distant cry
that distant cry
in darkness.

She wonders what is real and what is not.

If born of worm, a thing can live apart.

If it could ever come to know itself

And then she grows too tired to think at all

and so, exhausted,
falls again
to
sleep.

Sometimes she can hear the
children call,
she hears their voices in a
drug deaf dream.

Too scared to move, to eat,
create again
she rolls back into sleep
and all around the
holes
that she has left
the stars
fly out

She knows that somewhere
other lives begin
lives of night, of dark,
half-light and light.

And sometimes she can hear
the mystics call
she hears them murmur
through her sleepy dream
but all she knows is that she is
herself
a worm that grew
from nothing.

She hears them talk of sea
inside the fish

She feels the pain when men
pull out their guts
to find that deeper
meaning.

She knows that
knowledge is a weight
too much.
The worm creates but also it
destroys
although it only
means to know itself
perhaps, perhaps…
to love.

The worm is stirring,
turning distant dreams
that knock in snoring
breaks of sleep.
She hears the crow beak-crow feet
strange rain dance,
hears the distant music
of the beast,
hears the music of a beast
that sings,
tries to sing the music of
the primes.

Song calls the old worm up to make her
rise, calls her once again
to raise her head.

And so the worm awaits the
siren sound, the sound that
pulls through sand
through space
through time

When mystic and the
mathematician stand,
stand as one
and make a single sound,
a sound that rides the waving
of the primes,
the worm will push the pullover
of earth
and raise her head
and down will fall
a lava flow of hands
and those that call will fall
into her mouth
to see the place where all of
life began and man will know
his god and god his man.

Swimming in the gene pool
of our birth,
dancing to the music
of the memes,

when scientist and mystic
move as one,

when artists learn to ride
the waves of maths,

then we will find the song,
the siren song

the song that calls the worm

the song to sing us back
where we began.

Beyond
Sadness,
Beyond
Tears,
Beyond
Dusk
Beyond
Dark
Beyond
Silence
Beyond
Scream
A birthsong cries
on ears too deaf to hear.
Beyond
Sadness
Beyond
Tears
Beyond
Dusk
Beyond
Dark
Beyond
Silence
Beyond
Scream.

WONDERING SONGS

They asked the world
to sing its secret song
to open up the Bletchley Park
of life.

They asked the earth,
the water and the planets
if they would sing their song.
They answered them
with nothing.

Then the gardener
told the pruning
of the tree.

The midwife
told the welcome song
of life.

The man who prods
the drains with his long rod,
sang a song of affluence
and waste.

Tjuringas fell
on foreign ground.

Targes called the symbols
of their paint

churingas, drums and harps
all answered
in brush paint strokes
of silence.

And those who would know
mountains
asked the rock,

And those who would know Salmon
asked the water
that it tastes

The wheat
told all the stories
of the grain.

The stormcloud
told the cycle songs
of rain.

And rocks
drowning in torrents
of waves
spoke of the Earth
without music.

Strobing through the
journey of his years,
a man beside an open window
carves out his way
through the mountains.

The chessboard of life
may be battered
and the knight that we hold,
be chipped
but the checkmate of
imperfection is
final.

Deliver your ears
to the songs of creation,
take a tuning fork
to resonate the sound.

Can you hear, through
water and fire,
the chorus of wind
and of stone?

Only crow
who stands steadfast
on the shoulder of hope,
hears the cacophony
calling.

SONG OF THE DARK

I
am
the need of Sun.
Where light is not
where warmth has gone
I am the want of sight.

In lands of midday moons,
forgotten smiles,
I ride into the house
that sorrow calls.
My needles prick
the eyeballs of the night.

As lethargies of curtains
close their eyelids,
hold them tight.
I ride eternally
the scream of night.

I
am
the need of Sun,
the want of Light.

SONG OF MOUNTAIN MIST

When Alpha-Omega
ordered the old world's
awning

white was pure and black
sky knew no star
to portend warning.

Now tossed and blown in the
flux of a world's confusion,

indefinite
grey
flakes
fall

chilled by a new sun dawning.

VOLCANO SONG

When rage roars
and skies bleed
and lava flows
from the fault
that is
my mouth

they
run
for
cover.

Dawn's half light
bears witness to the burning of their soles.

The fakirs of man's family
take the walk
of a thousand coals.

Song of Ice

Days of darkness pass
as winter melts to spring.

Styling a head in first ice
he carves a frozen image.

Shielding his creation from the sun

he marvels that his
idol's coldness burns him.

Song of the Sea

Ssh, ssh,
they hear Atlantis call.

Ssh, ssh,
they motion to the sea.

Take me down to the sea again
to the sun and the sand and the sky,
where waves return to the primal womb
and sands kiss the sea goodbye

Ssh, ssh,
they hear Atlantis call.
Ssh, ssh,
they motion to the sea.

HARP SONG

I am the harp
that plays the wind of change.

Listen to my echo in your stillness.

You are the conch
that sings an ancient song.

Your music forms a fragile holding shell.

Your fingers roll my harp strings
turn my tides.

Help me tune these strings to play the world.

Write me notes to tell the earthy noise
that makes a man forget

the silent song
his call
the womb of days.

BIRTH SONG

I whispered to the stars
May all your dreams come true

I whispered to the moon
May her face shine down upon you

I whispered to the sea
to hold you in her arms

I whispered to the owl
to fill your nights with psalms

I whispered to the cockerel
to herald in your days

I whispered to the trees
to make a bridle for your ways

I whispered to the Earth
to ground you

I whispered to the Sun
to call you.

May the stars dream you,
moon shine you,
sea hold you,
wind reveal
the ringing of your
days.

SONG OF THE WHITE EAGLE

Live life with compassion,
a love that does not end.
Each man to you
a brother is,
each enemy
a friend.

Sex brings death
to challenge us
but love can interpose,
speak in tongues of men and angels,
seek the noumenon of rose.

The wind uplifts my feathers,
it flies beneath my wings.
We fly with grace, on certitude,
upon salvation's wings.

DOVES'S VOLVOX SONG

Happy volvox, tiny planet
kissed by the sun's long years
dancing in your orbit
to the music of the
Spheres.
The enigma of your origin
is scattered on the Earth,
peaceful sphere of emerald,
Oh, paradox of birth.

You purposely revolved
before the coming of the night.
The sama of the sufi
spins to see your sacred sight.
Zoologist and Botanist
both claimed you as their own.
You are one and you are many,
you are one, you are alone.

In Eden, time seemed endless
and all things were at home.
Eve, the budding virgin birth
to Adam, made sweet moan.
They were the glistening apple
but the hanging fruit seemed more
so they split themselves into their sex
and seed fell to the floor.

They longed to be much wiser,
coloured brighter by their sex,
doomed to wander into lands
where death reigned
terra rex.
And now they walk in shadow
catching glimpses of the sun.
They know and yet,
they do not know,
from memory they run.

And somewhere
on the tree of life
the sephirah they climb,
watch ten ox-herding pictures
walk a middle way
through time.

Memories grow distant
and knowledge fades away.
Sex inside a life becomes
a passing summer's day.

Remember self, like volvox,
when paradox strikes hot.
Of plant and animal it is
and yet, of both, it's not.

Man fell by choice
to climb again
the branches of the tree,
he bites upon the apple
of his curiosity.

Eve was not the villain,
it was written and was not,
that man must journey out
to find the treasure he has got.

Children are the seed of life,
not wages of some sin,
a serpent's trick,
a woman's smile,
don't end where they begin.

CROW WATCHES

Crow grew sick of watching,
of vomiting the boredom
of it up.

Deep inside him
something spoke itself.
Not words of crow or man
but wind that passes
through a mountain pass,
a
whistled
emptiness.

And where men journeyed
roads were lined with crows
to haunt and taunt them
with their power of signs.

Each bony skull
became a resting place
where wings from aeons aching
could find rest.

Somewhere inside the fog
of human minds
where mountain tops
are hidden or ignored
he pulled them from the safety
of their beds,
he flew them through
the consciousness of night,
not knowing if they travelled
or they slept,
not knowing if they dreamt
or were awake
lost in some strange resting place.

They saw the signs
but did not understand
until they heard
the melodies,
the songs of lullabies
the tunes that help the dreamers
to awake.

CROW IS SICK

Crow listened to the eagle.
He had heard
the robin singing
after death,
had grown sick
of words.

He remembered
how the volvox
had revolved.

He remembered
how the worm
was split   in two.

He remembered
all the potters and,
the Eden songs

Amoeba and paramecium,
immortal
until
sex.

The world begins from
boredom and of choice.

And what of word?
Who said the world's
a thing that word begat?

There were too many words...
too many words
and far too few
were worthy
of recall.

CROW'S VOLVOX SONG

Who drove a Volvo
through volvox, Derrida?
Who rolled the whey out of
whet-what-that?
Is it any wonder
words of thun*der rid a* world
of its dreams
in an act.

You found a *placet*,
erased the *non...*
is there some
significance in that?

Who put the *vol* into volvox,
Jacques?
Who gave it wings
that could fly?

Who heard the *vox*
of the volvox, Jack...
As this deconstructing world
rolls by.

Word
a word
in the beginning
in the beginning was
in the beginning was a
in the beginning was a word.
Once upon a time there was a
whisper of logos of a word
Chinese whispers of a word.
Whispers of a word
of a word
a word
word
in
evening
sky
Eden
sky
identify
identify
between the
I and Y
letters found
themselves
and
formed
a
word.

CROW ASKS WHY

Why do they try to write
down words at all?
Reaching down into their
hearts to pull the very
question of them out.
Why do they try to write
down words at all?

Rubbing on the ringing
of their glass
they hear a mantric Om
that sings them,
rings them
to a shattering of glass.
Why do they try to make
words sing at all?

Why do they fight the winds
that come to call?
Driving stakes into the
ground, their ropes are taut to
hold them in the green tents
of their lives.
Why do they fight the winds
that come to call?

Why can't they let the wind
within them out?
Canvas skinned with flat lips
that they purse to make a
whistle sound.
Why don't they bellow all the
wind sound out?

Bellowed by the yeasting
of their words
they sense the foreign winds
that move them,
hear the vortex build,
the tribal call.

Why do they try to fight
the wind
at all?
Why do they try
to write down words
at all?

CROW IS PUZZLED

Crow pecked into the
splintered skulls of men,
cast out runes of
question marks,
lay the questions out
in rows
on sand
pecked
and
pecked
and
tried
to
understand.
Pecked
and
pecked
and
tried
to
understand.

Crow became more troubled
and confused,
he wondered at the thoughts
and acts of men
who journeyed from their
darkness into light
and
into
deeper darkness.

He flew about the world
and watched them fight.
He watched them hate and hit
and hurt and shout:
treading on the shoulders
of the weak,
kicking out their way into
a space,
climbing up
the ladder of career,
powering the chain-saws
of their lives
to wipe a forest of
redemption
out.

Turning on the crow
they blamed the night,
they blamed the stars,
the portents and the signs.
They looked out in the world
to find the fault,
but never in the darkness
of themselves.

And then crow drilled
into
them
with his eye,
until they learned to look
inside
themselves,

for he had left the palace
of the skulls
and as he left
the blood of rivers bled
and as he flew
he knew
that he would find
new human heads
to crack
that he would rest
inside
the human head.

That he would
carve
a way
of
question marks.

And with his yellow eye
he drilled and drilled,
he watched and pecked
the talking sound of thoughts
rehearsed to find
the vox in him.
Until tomorrow, *Cras,*
Tomorrow, *Cras,*
he said

INSIDE THE BOWLER HAT

Inside their heads he hangs a
bowler hat.
Upturned it makes a haven of
a nest.
He stares out of the grey
clothed, grey eyed man
who hides behind a pink
'Financial Times.'

He pecks to find the boy
who rang the bell,
he pecks to find the climbed
forbidden wall,
he pecks to find the smarting,
scrumping knee,
he pecks to find the
Superman in tights.

Inside this carriage ride the
men in suits
inside their heads he's
pecking at their lives
through time and space
in lives like shopping bags
on tracks that run in parallel.

CROW THINKS HIMSELF INTO AN ICARUS

Crow flew like Icarus
into the sun.
He flew too fast
into the heat of it.
Charred his wings
and burnt his feathers black:
his charcoal feathers fuelled
the brightening sun.
The sockets of his eyes
were amber lights
a burn of ember eyes
that stared out from the blackness
of himself to keep a watch upon
eternity.

Where he had yawned the
aeons out through time.

CROW FLIES

From a mouth that yawns
an aeon's boredom out,
Crow flies

Like a cyclone
in the vortex of a doubt,
Crow flies

In a question mark
that hangs its feathers out,
Crow flies

A philosopher
who pecks his insides out,
Crow flies

On a Riemann wave
invisible-unheard,
Crow flies

From the snoring of a God
who seems absurd,
Crow flies

DOVE FLIES

In a search to find the Golden Mean of Dreams,
The Dove

With an olive branch of
paradigms and memes,
The Dove

Through the rainbow show,
of the small stitched silver seams,
The Dove

THEY DREAM OF JACOB'S LADDER

And in the deserts of their lives
the people climbed their
Jacob's ladder,
they pulled it up behind them.
Despaired that they would
ever speak again in words
of meaning.
They wondered if they had
ever really spoken,
ever really spoken much at all.
Definitions,
words and tools of Science,
talk of paradigms that only really work
until they fall.
They liked the crosswords'
clever cryptic clues,
then spewed up knowledge,
looked to find a carrot
of the truth.

They deconstruct, deduct
and then destruct.

MEN THINK THEIR WAY INTO BEING

To do is to be Descartes

Of the making of books
There is no end
And too much study
is a weariness of the flesh.

To be is to do Sartre

The Priest and the Prostitute
read their truths on the lavatory wall.

You are you and I am me
we live and move
quite separately.

You are me and I am you
dancing in
each other's
shoe.

Do be
do

CANDLE PROMISE

Snatched from our drawer
into darkness.

You were our unspent candle.

We must have known
that you were thirsty for the flame

and yet, you lie here now
with wick of white.

Was it in our wisdom
that they snatched you
from the safety of
a drawer?

Snuffed out your only chance
to see the light.

BARAK

Barak, Barak.
Roll your thunder
throw your lightning
bolt the night.

Barak, Barak.
Hear them calling
they are waiting.
Cast your light.

Barak, Barak.
Hear us whisper
you can hear all
left and right.

Barak, Barak.
Heal the fission
bring Love's vision
into sight.

Barak, Barak.
Strike their foreheads
let them see their
inner light.

The Priestess

The Priestess
rose her body from the chair,
struck the sceptre hard upon
the mound,
smiled a toothcomb waterfall
of light
to straighten up
the Cader Idris trail.
She gave the gift from Bethlehem
away
to one who fought the
vampire bite of night,
held out the cross of white
Mother of Pearl
to shield the child in sleep
until the day where
on the pews,
inside the strong Welsh walls
on the leafy beds by
waterfalls
the sun would kiss her
handmaiden
of light.

MAN AND WIFE

And the man in the
bowler hat
said,

'What I do not know
I will not say I know.'

'What I do not feel
I will not say I feel.'
A river's blood
slips
down
the
castle
steps

as the guts
of his wife
scream
from the knotsinthefloor.

She takes a tongue that is her dental probe
devised of raw emotion,
whittled
to the contours
of a beak,
perches on her husband's ear,
digs in her claws
pecks into the soft space
of his brain
demands his mind
to speak.

THE EAGLE

The eagle who had flown on
distant hills
listened to the
tales that crow had told.

He knew he was the *Vol,*
he understood his role.

He lifted up his head into the
skies and with his wings he
spanned eternity.

And as he flew
he chanted
words of crow.

Moving closer,
soaring into searing,
filling up the nostrils of the earth
with a golden feathered singe.
He flew.

This time there was no
blackened snow.

This time nothing fell,

except an eagle's whiteness
and a heat that blessed.
Light shone out the way of
compass points
and from the
ground,
a host of flying feathers
floated upwards.

HOPE SONG

Swimming in the gene pool
of their birth,
dancing to the music
of the memes
the scientist and mystic
move as one.

Artists learn to ride the waves of maths

Mathematicians solve the siren song,

find the song at last
that calls
the worm,

The song that sings us back
where we
began.

Ex Nihilo Nihil Fit

In the beginning was
the void.
A void, as is a void,
of but itself.
A formless emptiness
that sucks its own self in
and spews the changing
centre of it
out.

The void was of itself.
Each centre emptiness
was once spewed out.
Each outer emptiness
was once sucked in:
changing yet unchanging.

And thing became a thing
that was itself.
Unaware of patterns
that were forming.
Repeating patterns played
from outside in
and
then
from inside
out.

The void was in the part
and in the whole.

The void was in the pattern
now repeating.
And neither was there darkness nor the light,
but void.

When void had learnt the arkon
of itself,
when arkon stood
where arkon was
before

When consciousness in part
knew its whole self:
not as in the consciousness of men
but in a way that energy
works to find a way
to form
again

Inside blackness
shone the inner light
and in the light the blackness knew itself
and shuddered.

The energy of blackness
and of light was but the void
becoming.

When blackness knew the darkness
of itself
and light knew of the blinding
of its light
each took
a
different
path.

And energy that warmed
in its own light
and cooled inside the depths
of its own darkness
knew of its own self
in the becoming.

And darkness thought itself
a different thing.
And light shone out a separate
shining path
until they thought themselves
as things
quite   different.

Then the light wings
of the eagle
and the dark wings
of the crow
grew their shades of feathers
for the flying.

For the eagle and the crow
that were the same had come out of
the cosmic dancing dust,
had grown into two feathered things,
flying out of darkness,
flying out of darkness
into light.

SOME SAY
(I)

Some would say,
'Let people have their dreams;
sticky dreams that pull the tooth of night,

their Alpha wave of dreams
from strange machines,

their candle flames of dreams
that open up the dungeon's maze
and offer, for a while,
a certain sight,

let them have their cave of shadow
flickerings
their dirty windowed view
of distant light.

SOME WOULD SAY
(II)

Some would say
'Dream on,
for what are days?

Days are for walking the dog,
following
each winding path,
each wagging tail
or willow branch.
Days are for walking the dog.

Days are for throwing
small sticks,
retrieving pine cone
acorn cups
of tokens.
Days are for throwing small sticks.

DOVE'S LOVE SONG

'Our eyes cannot see it
Our ears cannot hear it
Our noses can't smell it
Our mouths cannot taste it
Our senses can't feel it
Or mind understand it

What value is on it?
All pride falls upon it.
Our essence of it
Our being grows in it
The selflessness of it
The quiddity of it
A blessing upon it
And all those who give it

Pure love'

LIFE WOULD BE SO EASY

Life would be so easy if it wasn't for the clock.
If it wasn't for the tricking of a hot, sharp clicking,
of the second hand slipping,
of a time piece.

Life would be so simple.
If it wasn't for a small face hanging from its chain
hovering the plugging place, above the choking drain,
peeping from the pocket of an old man's suit
as it moves its peep-ho hands across
the clockface.

Life would be so simple if it wasn't for the winding down
Of days, for theBlack Dog barking, for the
Crowblack, slow back beating of a Time Lord's wings.

Life would be so easy
if it wasn't for the time piece,
clockface
keyhole
Lording of those
keyholelording of those eyes.

MANKIND LISTENS FOR THE HORSEMEN

And sometimes people sing their fear of death.

With just five minutes left
what will you do?

Conjure like old Prospero
your books.

Cook the red marked losses
on the light white paper weighing
of your balance sheet

With just five minutes left what will you do?

Will you look into
the lion's mouth
at death?

Will you sprinkle from an empty cellar
crystals of a salt of truth?
Try to sell the horsemen
raffle tickets for
a dance with death,
tell the horsemen
it never was your fault.
Ariel – a fairy too ethereal
Caliban - too crass to merit trust
Gave you no honest chances
to show your worth
on Earth.

Perhaps you'll file a suit to sue
the eternal coatman.
Who, if he had done his job
would have made you face the fact that
one day you would die.
You really can't be blamed,
it's not your fault.

With just five minutes left what will you do?

Caught inside a cosmic tempest's eye
searching through your pockets
for prescriptions that just didn't help
to clear that sticky problem in your eye.

With just five minutes left what will you do?

When you're asked
to tell the measure of your life,
will you blame the mix up
of a metric world
when you were born
to measurements Imperial?

With just five minutes left what will you do?

Will you try one tiny last white lie
to tippex out the errors of your life?

With just five minutes left
What will you do...

Fear falls fast as the eagle flies
with talons taut and prying eyes
and we poor creatures run and hide
safe in the hollows of our lives.

Man sheds his skin
in days and years
in spent desires
and childhood fears

skins that grow
from new year fears
must have a baby's face.

And will you call the footman,
butler, servant?
Tell him when it's time to hold your
coat.
Each page must know its place.

And if he must,
then he may hold the door -
When you are ready -
not before.

With just five minutes left
What will you do?

Between the dream of day
And the walk of the night
there is sometimes
a

space

a tiny place
of
meditation.

MINACK

Minack,
Minack,
Meditation
Muses sing to me.

Incantation
Inspiration
In perpetuity.

Nights of Numbness,
Nocturne
Neume.
Nestled by the sea.

Ampitheatre by Rowena. New
Antiquity.

Cornish waters
Calling waters
Cerinthus – be done.

Knowledge – Gnosis
Strange hypnosis
Sophistry and sun.

CROW YAWNS

Crow is yawning out
another ache,
an emptiness so very much
like death,
a sorrow screaming out
a silent pain.
My body is the going out
of breath.

All day I feel the readiness
of flight,
a weave of sighs that
dolphins out the air.
A tidal mourning of a
whale's lament
that echoes out the echo
of despair.

And yet there is no rain,
there is no rain.
The eagle tears will fall one day,
not yet.
Crow treads upon the vellum
of a pain
that our small senses
easily forget.

The mighty worm is turning
once again
and labouring through love
another light.

Crow vomits out the boredom
of a day
and something good is leaving us
tonight.

WHERE IS THE GULF OF HEAVEN?

Where is the Gulf of Heaven?
Is it in this solid place?

Where is the Gulf of Heaven?
Somewhere in the country
or the town?

Where is the Gulf of Heaven?
Beyond the sparrowhawks,
the spacemen and the crane?

Where is the Gulf of Heaven?
Somewhere in the shornings
of the gorse and of the fern
where farmers roll Welsh
hillsides into
carpets.

Where is the Gulf of Heaven?
Far off beyond the beachless sea.

Where is the Gulf of Heaven?
In the red grass cool fired
words on a board writing
their way into whiteness.

Where is the Gulf of Heaven?

Where the mirror of the sky
can see its face and the wind
hears the whisper of its name.

Where is the Gulf of Heaven?
On this uneven ground
pitched between the feather
and the stone.
Cradled by the Berwyns and
the Dee there is a children's stream
where laughter runs
all morning.

ANOTHER EVOLUTION

Swim drowned out of
solipsistic swamps like
children out of depth
with arms too weak
who reason up a toe,
a foot, a knee,
contort their bodies up
onto a bank.

We mind grab other theories,
other thoughts,
grip the roots that anchor pull
our thoughts,
heave-ho out
onto some solid place
where feet imagine ground
that knows no space
between the moving matter
of the Earth,
between the quark and quarklet,
coloured scientific bits too small
for even microscopes to find,
too great for shrinking minds to understand.

And then we fall,
exhausted
into sleep
between the roots
that used to seem so firm,
the roots that never moved
beneath the Earth
move over, under,
through us in our sleep;
weave through ears and brains
to enter dreams
where they, no longer earthbound,
weave a way,
shoot their tendrils up
into the stars,
weave the veins and arteries
of Man,
dance the fluid movements
into sky,
weave a matrix tapestry
of life.

THE PROPHETESS

Throat dry in the calling I came to you
remembering Hagar's dragging feet,
the ribboned flesh,
the red of blood on rock.

Sunblind, sun burnt into seeing
I heard your simple trumpets sound,
felt the wind from the wings
as the Seraphim rejoiced.

You opened every cell of me
flung wide each door,
licked clean each fibre
from each hermit floor
and walked me through this marathon
of aching.

Why were there never neon signs
to welcome and to guide me
at the crossing place.

Oh let your angel's kisses burn your vision
on my eyes.
I am clasped inside the crook of
of an eagle's claw
and fly through sea and soil,
through land and vine
on the break of a quantum wave
to be those things that I was once before.

Tear from my mouth this babbling tongue
with the might of your messenger's hand
numbing my lips with the venom of a snake
split my breast in two with
your shining sword.
Let me watch this organ of my heart
beat inside Love's hand.

My chest is a thousand sparks,
a burning coal,
my ribs are now the cradle of your lullaby.
Let me hear the wind songs call the desert sand.

'Arise now Prophetess
and see
let all men know my will through thee,
overland and over sea,
through eagle spanned eternity.
Sear the hearts of my people.
Let my people feel the wind
within my word.'

BELOVED

From that first morning song
you must have known
that I would drive
these choking roads
to find
you.

And now I come

not comically
as a child waddling his father's wellies
on a dew wet grass,

not meekly as the young
betrothed who learns to say
'Amen.'

Not dreamily climbing up
the ladder of another's sleep.

Nor do I come barefoot,
bravely
fast racing the spearhead
chasing on an arrow's
flight,

but with shell to my left and
pen of a sword to my right
heart's embers fanned
by your eyes shining the faces
of strangers.

I come to you slowly
following the trail of the
pony path

A
woman
wet-socked
walking.

WAYS OF KNOWING

Who could ever know
dreams come
to this?

From three dawn kitchen-chatted
dreams of crow
there came a living bird,
with body large,
who banged upon the window
of our glass
and burn drilled with his eye
into my skull
until he found a place
where he could roost.

Then there came the tapping
from inside,
the tap-tap-tapping
out of inner eye,
and through the holes he
bored, the winds swept
through.

Crow pecked and ate each dark
policing thought,
swallowed worm restrictions
of the mind,
opened up a trust that flies
the wind and blows through
Guernos, Beaulieu,
Heptonstall near Hebden
Bridge, Iona, Minack,
Criccieth and rests south east
of Snowshill's
Cotswold
walls.

It dolphin loops the lichen
Rannoch air, dives the
intuition of the sea,
Dreams the Llanfinangel
waterfall,
Raises up a sceptre on the
mound to straighten up the
Cader Idris tale.

Against an ancient abbey's
older tree I knew the earth
had called you down to sleep
and blessed your path.
The eagle of Dalchreichat
sign was strong and words
that came too soon,
were whispered now,
whispered in that last fog
flying sleep.

Before we took the train, I
knew you'd gone,
knew that you flew strongly
in the end and in the warming
sun, had found your resting
place.

Crow had pecked the barriers
of thought and suddenly I
saw those other signs,
the birdsong of a world that
flies its course greeted by the
robin after death,
the magpie messenger and
then the crow,
an eagle purity in Scottish
sky.

But there was nothing
brighter than the crow
whose dark form cried a
hope song through the sky.

'Tomorrow, *cras*
tomorrow, *cras*
we fly.'

SNOWSHILL: A PARTING (I)

No great Castaneda tale of
power flew down

no Nietzschian slave morality
was culled

this crow was not a Matthew
Sweeney ghost,

no alien film of feathers
pushed through pores

no cawed, 'Good Morning,'
came

no husband's scream.

The metamorphosis – not
Kafkaesque...

Crow simply built himself a
little nest.

He nestled in the cave that
was my skull

and opened up another path
to see.

And when he left
there was no bottled wine,

no green eyed monster drove
him to a wall

even when the strangers built
a road that crunched the
ancient Oak

he did not find convenient
excuse to make a show of
going.

At Snowshill, he left... slowly.

SNOWSHILL: A PARTING (II)

Will it end now, crow?
Tell me
will it end?

Seven countries
in as many days.

Your coming filled the silent
bell of Ghent.

Your feathers turned to
whiteness there at Rheims
before the great cathedral's
coloured glass.

There are no shell signs hidden
on this path.

No strident yellow arrows
show your shadow
slipping from me.

Your yellow eye
looks out from night's dark
corners.

I have held you through these
last few hectic years,
have hummed your way
to sleep and watched your show
of nightmares.
'Remember Pandemonium,
the silver net of dreams,' you said.
I have tried, but Crow,
I grow so tired.

They make new targets of
our Babel Towers

and say they know their
God.
God, help us all.

No gentle man would usher in,
too soon,
another's death.

What sacrifice is this
that turns love
cold?

Is this it?

Is this where we shall end?

Is this where wanderings of days
will cease?

Those grey clouds
mark the backcloth
of a rookery

nesting there
a murder of
your friends.

A great
Crow Watch
is listening.

To my right
I hear the dovecote's
whispered innocence.

But, crow,
my flesh is tired
of all the signs

my eyes have read
too many
worthy books

decoded myths
so often misconstrued
and now I see the Zenith
lies
South East

and so do you.
There is no North to fear, no
East or West
a conifer grows from the
flower's heart.

This flower of bishop's hats in
Cotswold stone are offering
more symbols and more
signs.

St Bernard loved the virgin
and the tree, his sermon on
humility is written here in
steps.

But now I'm tired of books
and chasing signs.

You leave my head and fly
back to your tree

Some other mind will share
your visions, crow.
Will bring you rest.

As you fly off I read your
parting sign
beside the clock:

'Aura Capitas'

And I am free
To be a Basho frog
jumping
in
an
Agapaic pool

CROW'S LAST FLIGHT

Crow,
fly out again,
fly on and up,
fly out like
Icarus.

Fly out fast
into the heat of it.
Let the charring of your
charcoal feathers brighten up
a sun fuelled burning.
The sockets of your eyes
are amber lights
embers burnt from blackness
of the self.
An eye
that is the hub
inside the clockspin
of eternity.

Crow,
fly out again.
Fly upwards,
fly your blackened feathers
into light.

MANTILLA LAMENT

And is it true, father?
Is it true what you said
that the dead will walk out
with their hands in the hands
of the dead?

And did you
know that he would
come?

And did you
know what he would
say?

And are you
smiling?

There was morphine
in the glove seat
of the long drive home
and now there are questions
for the asking.

'It's a shame,' you said,
'to be leaving.'

In your scattering of atoms,
can you feel me?

Do you believe in a life
before death?

Or are we all
forgotten?

Grief is far too great a shape
to bend to fortune,
too large a scream for clichés
or for cards.

And the world is much too loud
and colours much too bright.

Today I walk on the unmown grass
and I remember you.
Today the cupboard door
hangs down its wing
and it remembers you.

And I wonder if thoughts are heard
or if words are all wasted to silence.

In my nose -
peardrops
breathe.

On my tongue -
the small pink petal
of a rose.

And of the making of books
there is no end
and, yes, too much study is
a weariness of
the flesh,

and yet,
they write.

and yet,
we write.

And yet,
I write.

Oh, for the being of it.
Oh, for the believing,
without seeing, of it.

And,
Oh, Abba,
Oh, Abba,
Oh, Abba, Abba, Abba, Oh.

Oh,
for the cradle song.
Oh,
for the Mama-Papa
cradle of the night,
for the carol after death
that tells us that it knows now
it was right.

I will not fear the watch
of ivory towers,
the men whose words
of references
tie up their bows of
endings.
I will swirl my skirts to whirl
in sparks of light.

There are promises to keep
before the night.

My mantilla is black and gold,
my mantilla is black and gold.
My mantilla is
black for the mourning -
gold for the shining,
my mantilla is
black and gold.

In the night's thin veil
is a world before words
before sentence formed
and world grew far too heavy-
sound swirled,
consciousness whirled
and the moon
was a laugh
in an eye.
Now an aeroplane charters
an ancient path
in the silk of
a Samhain sky,
and a priest in Beijing
in his Temple of Heaven
stands with his hands to the sky,
offering a prayer for good harvest.

And the wood of the circles that hold him
knows no nails.

THE HOUSEWIFE DANCES

At first light
she is gathering sticks.

sweeping the step
with her brush and a pan,

scrubbing the step with a
bristling brush.

All morning
she's down on her knees,

her hand shines the grate
in its rhythm of fast moving
circles.

And the hearth is a mirror
of all that she shines
with the dance of a duster
so soft.

And the morning is spent
on her knees.

Soon she will walk up the stairs,
she will rise to the beds,
she will shake from the pillows
a feathering fall.

Ssh
Ssh

Hear the laughter that screams
in a feather down fall

Ssh
Ssh

Hear her song as it climbs up
the dry waterfall

Ssh
Ssh

In a trance she will dance out her life
on her knees, on her knees.
In a trance
she will dance out her life.

DAWN OF THE FIRST DAY

The night, yet not the night,
the dawn of that first dream
was strange.

I could not understand
why that sincere
and unassuming man
would weave his silver cord
inside my dream.

Had all this happened
only in the mind?
Surely dreams are only
minds unfolding.

And yet it seemed
that rather than my
bringing his face in,
he had in some way
summoned me upon
a journey out.

I had no wish to cause
offence

but felt that I must
speak the truth.

*I do not understand your
words,* I said.

Read them again
and then again,
he said.

Startled by the morning light
I found myself awake and
wished to pull my husband
from his sleep,
but did not.

And when at last he yawned
himself awake
I told him of that
strangest dream
not surreal, unreal

in black or white
but coloured with the detail
of the world:

A kitchen table, cosy and
familiar,
a kitchen chat,
the warm and wooden table top
firmly felt beneath
an open palm.

The voice that said it knew
now it was right,
before the academic stuff.
At least, in part, it knew now
it was right.

The eyes that were so gentle
but intense.

The parting plea:
Please tell my wife
I know now I was right.. not
wrong..half-right..
in part, at least
I know now
I was right.

My husband spoke of
catalogues and thoughts
of how the brain
imagines things.

Our dreams, it seems, are
nothing but a jumble sale,
a sleeping stall of oddments
sorted out.

And so all day the dream
was locked away:

an envelope behind the clock,
a key beneath a flower pot,
a cobweb in the corner of the
cupboard woven in the
darkness of that world
beneath the stairs.

And in my hand a duster
gently wiped
And in the sink the crocks
were washed,
piles of junk were shifted,
sorted, moved.

The day was spent in sorting
out the objects of the house.
An odd socks hunt.
A Spring time type of
sorting.

DAWN OF THE SECOND DAY

On the second day there
came upon the dawn
a second dream.

This time I tried to pinch
myself awake
was conscious of it all:
the journey out,
the tables chairs,
the texture and the warmth
of wood, the smell of
something in a place
I did not recognise,
the jarring of a suit
and someone's eyes,
a blue and brown
I can't remember quite.

The voice was just the same
gentle but intense and
creeping from the half-house
of a smile.

Talking of a raven or a crow,
his voice grew more intense
until at last I thought of one
small book bought for just
one pound some twenty years ago.

Where was it now?
Lost or cloaked in dust on
some high shelf.

I'd had no need to look.
I did not know.

But though I told myself
I only dreamt,
I still felt it was wrong
to cause offence
so did not say I'd never read
more than a tenth of it.
Instead I asked,
Why should I read this book?
I'm sure I'll never
understand

a word of it.
At this, he only smiled
a patient smile
Read Crow, read Crow
he said.

And as I felt myself pulled
from his sight,
I heard him say

Please tell my wife,
please tell her I was right.

His words had left an echo
in my head,
my eyes took in the clock
where fingers pointed
my returning:-
quarter to six
hands on a clock face read.

Before the dream
the clock said half past five.
At quarter to six
the clock showed my returning.

It seemed that I had walked
a tunnel's light
and yet had never really left
this bed.
I thought of minds that are a
maze, a labyrinth of images
to walk and waited for my husband
to awake. I told him of the second dream
then spent the day in
unaccustomed cleaning.

DAWN OF THE THIRD DAY

The third night came and
with it came the dawn.
The kitchen and the table
were the same.

An urgency betrayed
the patient voice
but I was stubborn,
ground in common sense.

Life is tangible and dreams
are not.
How can a mind be
bullied into books?

The house was cleaned
apart from dusty shelves.

The story of the dream stayed
there, in walls.
Who in their right mind
lets such stories out?

CROW KNOCKS

Three dawns had come and
with them came three dreams.

And now there came a
banging noise so loud it knocked
the snoring of the house
awake.

At half past five,
just as the dreams before,
I heard my son call
Come now,
Come,
Come ... look at this.

His father, in the way of
those who sleep, felt for
slippers, followed them
to walk.

And there outside the
window
pressed against the glass,
the eye of a black crow,
staring.

It stared and stared
and then it flew away.

Later
it returned,
banged upon the window
once again.
It stared intently with the eye
of crow.
Quarter to six, the black bird
flew away.

At dawn, for seven days,
the black crow came,
banging on the window of the
room, staring in before it flew
away...only to return
and stare some more.

The crow would not be
satisfied with bread.
He would not leave until
we heard his call,
until we came to see his
staring eye.
He heard us talking
circles of coincidence.
We questioned those three
dreams and all the signs...
and would not read
or find the small blue book.

For seven days the black
crow would return at half
past five only to fly away,
return again and stare its
eye into the glass
at quarter to six
before it flew away
I almost thought
I'd heard it say goodbye,
but did not.

For seven days the large
black figure flew,
he banged to break the
sleeping house awake.
He pressed his yellow eye
against the glass.
He called and called
and called us out from sleep.

But not one cawing noise
slipped from its beak,
not one single *cras* of crow
escaped.
Its body banged into the pane
of glass.
Banged and banged
then banged and banged
again.

And on the seventh day when
crow returned,
pulled in by
the yellow of his eye,
there was a strange,
but understood
communion

A song that sang the rippling
of birth
a birth that sprang the
rippling of time
the gateway of a road where
signs would wait,
had opened.

That morning as I walked
beneath the tower,
that morning as I left
the cottage walls to walk
across the car park to the hall,
the crow came out of nowhere,
out of sky.
And flying in three circles
wove the silent threading of a last
goodbye.

Goodbye,
I might not understand.
Goodbye,
I'll try to understand,
Goodbye,
I hope to understand,
Goodbye.